DOUBLE
SNAPS

ALSO BY 2 BROS. & A WHITE GUY, INC.: *SNAPS*

DOUBLE SNAPS

JAMES L. PERCELAY, STEPHAN DWECK, AND MONTERIA IVEY

② BROS. & A WHITE GUY, INC.

QUILL
WILLIAM MORROW
NEW YORK

It is the policy of William Morrow and Company, Inc., and its imprints and affiliates, recognizing the importance of pre-serving what has been written, to print the books we publish on acid-free paper, and we exert our best efforts to that end.

Library of Congress Cataloging-in-Publication Data

Percelay, James.
  Double snaps / James Percelay, Stephan Dweck, Monteria Ivey.
    p.   cm.
  ISBN 0-688-14011-4
  1. Afro-Americans—Language (new words, slang, etc.).
  2. English language—United States—Terms and phrases.
  3. Afro-American wit and humor. 4. Afro-Americans—
  Quotations. 5. Quotations, American. 6. Black English.
  7. Americanisms. 8. Invective. I. Dweck, Stephan. II. Ivey,
  Monteria. III. Title.
  PE3727.N4P44   1995
  427'.973'08996—dc20   94-24792
                                                   CIP

Printed in the United States of America

First Edition

1 2 3 4 5 6 7 8 9 10

INTERIOR PHOTOGRAPHS BY KRISTINE LARSEN
BOOK DESIGN BY ELIZABETH VAN ITALLIE

Thanks to my family; twin brother, Bruce Andrew; NOL;

and Aunt Phyllis

—JAMES L. PERCELAY

To my parents, Abe and Mildred; Kendall Minter;

Claude Ismael; Jim Grant; and Larry Dais

—STEPHAN DWECK

To my loving mother, Ollie Ivey;

and to my fellow brothers and sisters in comedy

—MONTERIA IVEY

To our editor, Will Schwalbe,

who made writing this book a snap

SPECIAL THANKS FOR THE CONTINUED SUPPORT OF:

Bridget Potter, Betty Bitterman, Jon Rubin,

and the snappers at HBO

ALSO THANKS TO:

Judy McGrath, Doug Herzog, Abbie Turkhulie,

and the gang at MTV

THE DARK SNAPPER CREATED BY:

Hype Comics

CONTRIBUTING EDITORS:

Michelle Cuccuini, Sonya McLaughlin, and Maria Vecchione

ADDITIONAL SNAPS WRITTEN BY:

Sam Silver, Capital Jay, and Wil Sylvince

WE APPRECIATE THE KINDNESS OF THESE PEOPLE:

Gary Sharfin, Janice Young, Zack Schisgal,

Kevin Swain, Chester Mapp, A. Merrill Percelay (for the title),

and our agent, Mary Evans.

PREFACE

SNAPPING, our sources tell us, has spread beyond school playgrounds and into offices and dinner conversations, and is rumored to be practiced by a certain president from Arkansas. Snapping has been featured in TV programs on HBO, MTV, and Fox, and in commercials ranging from Nike sneakers to Hallmark cards. *The Tom Snyder Show* has covered the growth of snapping, as has CNN, *Vanity Fair*, *Entertainment Weekly*, and *The Wall Street Journal;* there's even a snaps computer bulletin board on Prodigy.

Who doesn't savor the satisfaction of putting that special someone in his or her place—whether it's the arrogant salesperson in a clothing store or the jerk driving fifteen miles per hour on the highway? Snapping, or "playing the dozens," was originally created by slaves to vent their hostilities without fear of their master's reprisal. Without diminishing the seriousness of the game's origins or its status as part of the African American cultural heritage, it remains a good way to let off steam in the 1990s.

It's the punch in the punch line that makes snapping so much fun and so effective. Nevertheless, the game ought to be played with care. *Double Snaps* is for serious snapping. After releasing our first book, *Snaps*, we received bags of snaps from across the country. The caliber of these verbal bullets was as if to say, "You guys think you know how to snap? These are *real* snaps!" So we loaded the chambers of this second book with snaps that are *doubly* rough as those in our first book. In fact, we added a chapter called "Nasty Snaps" just to contain these industrial-strength insults. And to avoid any litigation resulting from their improper use, we have included pictorial instructions in a chapter titled "Moves and Stances for Advanced Snapping." We're covered.

The snaps in this book came from a cross section of people who shared their favorite snaps, including cops, cabbies, kids, and *Snaps* readers from across the country. In addition, a number of writers created some original snaps for us. We have acknowledged the contributors in the back of the book. Within the chapters, we credited the remaining snaps when they came from a comedian, actor, D.J., musician, athlete, book, or TV show. The comedians are identified by name only. We gave a little more information on the rest.

Dr. Geneva Smitherman's piece on the history and contemporary significance of snapping explains the cultural importance of snapping as a valued African American creation and tradition. The letters you wrote us about snapping illustrate her points about the game's vitality. We have both enjoyed *and answered* all your letters; they have helped us keep connected to the game as it's practiced in different parts of the country. We would like to hear from more readers and can be reached at the address on page 176.

P.S. If comic books are your thing, we suggest you first catch up on the snapping superhero in "The Amazing Adventures of the Dark Snapper," page 164.

CONTENTS

13

AN INTRODUCTION TO THE
ART OF THE SNAP

IF I'M LYIN,
I'M FLYIN

BY DR. GENEVA SMITHERMAN

Yo' mama don't wear no draws
Ah seen her when she took 'em off
She soaked 'em in alcohol
She sold 'em tuh de Santy Claus
He told her 'twas against de law
To wear dem dirty draws.
—FROM ZORA NEALE HURSTON, *THEIR EYES WERE WATCHING GOD*[1]

I BET YOU a fat man against the hole in a doughnut that Hip-Hoppers think they invented "yo momma" jokes. Well, yall better ask somebody cause the game has been around in the Black Oral Tradition for generations, even long before Sista Zora included this little "yo momma" rhyme in her 1937 novel. "Oral Tradition"—which is also a part of the cultural experience of other groups such as Native Americans—refers to verbal games, stories, proverbs, jokes, and other cultural productions that have been passed on from one generation to the next by word of mouth. In Black America, this tradition preserves and celebrates African culture, which was adapted to a new way of life in America. Because Africans in America play with and on the Word, good talkers become heroes and she-roes. Bloods

1. Zora Neale Hurston, *Their Eyes Were Watching God*, first published in 1937. This excerpt is from the Perennial Library edition, ed. Henry Louis Gates, Jr. (New York: Harper & Row, 1990), p. 149. The novel is based on Hurston's fieldwork research while she was living in rural Florida, from about 1927 to 1932.

who can talk and testify, preach and prophesy, lie and signify, get much props. Enter *Double Snaps* and the aesthetics of the dis.

Literally speaking, when you "dis" someone, you discount, discredit, disrespect that person—a dis is an insult.[2] In the Black Oral Tradition, however, a dis also constitutes a verbal game, played with ritualized insults. The disses are purely ceremonial, which creates a safety zone. Like it's not personal, it's business—in this case, the business of playing on and with the Word.

There are two kinds of disses. One type is leveled at a person's mother (and sometimes at other relatives). Traditionally, this was referred to as "the dozens" (or "playin the dozens"). The other kind of dissin is aimed at a person or a thing, either just for fun, or to criticize that person or thing. This was referred to as "signifyin." Today, the two types of dissin are being conflated under a more general form of play, which we may refer to as "snaps," an emerging term for the game. (Other older terms for this ritualized insult tradition

2. Geneva Smitherman, *Black Talk: Words and Phrases from the Hood to the Amen Corner* (Boston: Houghton Mifflin, 1994), p. 94.

are "joanin," "cappin," "soundin," and "droppin lugs.")

Back in the day, virtually everybody in the Black community would, from time to time, engage in signifyin. But if you tried to go to "yo momma," some folk would tell you quick, "I laugh and kid, but I don't play" (meaning, "I don't play the dozens"). Perhaps, as 1960s political activist Hubert ("Rap") Brown wrote: "Signifying is more humane. Instead of coming down on somebody's mother, you come down on them."[3] That, of course, was another era, when women were put on pedestals and mothers were considered sacred. Today, the role of women has undergone a fundamental change, which helps to explain why the traditional distinction between "signifyin" and "the dozens" is blurring. However, let us here sing no sad songs for the demise of that old-timey image of women; it was false and oppressive. As a woman and as a mother, I'm wit the change. So in the game of snappin, if you play, either you or yo momma got to pay.

Generally, the dozens involves insults of mothers, but on occasion,

3. From Hubert ("Rap") Brown's autobiography, *Die Nigger Die!* (New York: Dial Press, 1969), p. 27.

players will bring in fathers, grandmothers, and other kinfolk. Sista Zora once referred to the dozens as "low-rating the ancestors of your opponent."[4] Richard Wright's 1963 novel, *Lawd Today*, portrays one of the funniest dozens contests I've ever read or heard. Al, Jake, and two of their partners are playin the dozens during a card game. Al reaches back five generations to Jake's "greatgreatgreat-*great* grandma . . . a Zulu queen in Africa. She was setting at the table and she said to the waiter: 'Say waiter, be sure and fetch me some of them missionary chitterlings. . . .' "[5] But, like Langston Hughes's folk character Jess B. Simple said, "Most Black folk don't play the Dozens that far back."

The game was and is played by all ages and by males and females. One-upmanship is the goal of this oral contest, best played in a group of appreciative onlookers, who are secondary participants in the game. They provide a kind of running commentary, repeating a really clever dis or interjecting responses like "Did yall hear that?,"

4. Zora Neale Hurston, "Story in Harlem Slang," *The American Mercury*, Vol. 55, No. 223 (1942), p. 96.
5. Richard Wright, *Lawd Today* (New York: Walker and Company, 1963), p. 81.

"Oh, shit!," "Oooooweee!," etc. The audience, with its laughter, high fives, and other responses, pushes the verbal duel to greater and greater heights of oratorical fantasy.

So, whassup with this game? Ain it kinda weird to be talkin bout "yo momma" this and "his momma" that—for fun?

For a people trying to survive under an oppressive racist yoke, the dozens provided a way, to borrow from Ralph Ellison, to "change the joke."[6] The game functioned as an outlet for what countless blues people and Jess B. Simple folk called "laughing to keep from crying."[7] It was a form of release for the suppressed rage and frustrations that were the result of being a Black man or woman trapped in White America. Despite economic discrimination and racist assaults

6. In his 1958 *Partisan Review* essay, "Change the Joke and Slip the Yoke," Ralph Ellison argued that the "Negro American folk tradition . . . has . . . much to tell us of the faith, humor and adaptability to reality necessary to live in a world which has taken on much of the insecurity and blueslike absurdity known to those who brought it into being." From Ralph Ellison's collection of essays, *Shadow and Act* (New York: Random House, 1964), pp. 58–59.

7. Jess B. Simple is a Harlem folk hero created by Langston Hughes during World War II, who became the subject of hundreds of stories that displayed African American humor and mother wit. The best stories from Hughes's several books about Simple are collected in Langston Hughes, *The Best of Simple* (New York: Hill and Wang, 1961).

against your personhood, you could ill afford to be hot; the dozens taught you how to chill. As well, the game taught discipline and self-control; it was a lesson in how to survive by verbal wit and cunning rhetoric, rather than physical violence. Ultimately, though, somebody got to lose. What then? Well, the dozens possesses the kind of humor that makes you laugh so hard you cry. A loser is thus provided with a face-saving way out—blending right on in with the loud laughter of the group. Today, the dozens, with its infusion into other cultures, still serves as a release from the pressures of daily existence, a safe, nonviolent method of venting hostility and suppressed rage within acceptable confines. Surely a healthier alternative than the rat-tat-tat-tat of glocks, domestic abuse, and other kinds of violence raging throughout *all* communities today.

The origin of the dozens, both the term and the game itself, remains debatable. Space does not permit a full discussion of the various theories; interested readers should consult the several references given in the footnote below.[8] Here I shall briefly discuss the most plausible theory, which relocates the game to the several cultures of Africa from which Black Americans came.[9] For example, in a

Bantu group in East Africa, described in a 1951 account, joking insults, such as "Eat your mother's anus," were observed among friends, and the Efik in Nigeria used ritualized insults such as "child of mixed sperm" (that is, you have more than one father, in other words, your mother is a ho). This theory about the dozens, which has been advanced by Melville Herskovits and others, is consistent with what we know about the history of African people in the

8. Middleton A. Harris, *The Black Book* (New York: Random House, 1974), p. 180; Geneva Smitherman, *Talkin and Testifyin: The Language of Black America* (Boston: Houghton Mifflin, 1977; reissued in paperback by Wayne State University Press, 1986), pp. 128–34; John Dollard, "The Dozens: Dialectic of Insult," *The American Imago*, Vol. I, No. 1 (November 1939), pp. 3–25; Roger D. Abrahams, *Deep Down in the Jungle* (Hatboro, PA: Folklore Associates, Inc., 1964), pp. 47–63.

9. Melville J. Herskovits, in *Funk and Wagnalls Standard Dictionary of Folklore, Mythology and Legend*, Vol. I (New York: Funk and Wagnalls, 1949), p. 322; David Dalby, "The African Element in American English," in Thomas Kochman, ed., *Rappin' and Stylin' Out: Communication in Urban Black America* (Urbana: University of Illinois Press, 1972) pp. 170–186. The reference to the West African origin of the dozens appears on p. 183; Joseph E. Holloway and Winifred K. Vass's *The African Heritage of American English* (Bloomington: Indiana University Press, 1993) seeks to "correct the mistaken assumption that only West Africans had a linguistic influence on African-American culture" (p. xiii) by demonstrating the influence from the languages of Central Africa. However, they follow Dalby's lead and attribute the "yo momma" phrase to West Africa (p. 145); Dudley Kidd, *Savage Childhood* (London, 1906), p. 198; Philip Mayer, "The Joking of 'Pals' in Gusii Age-Sets," *African Studies*, Vol. 10 (1951), pp. 27–41; Donald C. Simmons, "Possible West African Sources for the American Negro 'Dozens'," *Journal of American Folklore*, Vol. 76 (1963), pp. 339–40; William Elton, "Playing the Dozens," in "Miscellany," *American Speech*, Vol. 25, No. 1 (1950), pp. 230–33; William Schechter, *The History of Negro Humor in America* (New York: Fleet Press, 1970), pp. 11–13.

so-called "New World." Since culture is artifacts as well as the way people behave and think, it is logical that Africans in enslavement would tap into remembered cultural practices and verbal rituals from home and adapt them to life in a strange land.[10] From the git-go, the insult game would have been played in the slave communities, eventually taking on the English name "the dozens."

The dozens existed literally in the *Oral* Tradition until the first known written documentation in 1891. In a folk song collected in Texas, there are these lines:

> Talk about one thing, talk about another;
> But ef you talk about me, I'm gwain to talk about your mother.[11]

10. See, for example, Carter G. Woodson, *The African Background Outlined* (Washington, D.C.: Association for the Study of Negro Life and History, 1936); Melville J. Herskovits, *The Myth of the Negro Past* (Boston: Beacon Press, 1941), and *The New World Negro* (Bloomington: Indiana University Press, 1966); John W. Blassingame, *The Slave Community* (New York: Oxford University Press, 1972); Ivan Van Sertima, "My Gullah Brother and I: Exploration into a Community's Language and Myth Through Its Oral Tradition," in *Black English: A Seminar*, eds. Deborah Sears Harrison and Tom Trabasso (Hillsdale, N.J.: Erlbaum Associates, 1976); LeRoi Jones, *Blues People* (New York: William Morrow, 1963); Alfred B. Pasteur and Ivory L. Toldson, *Roots of Soul: the Psychology of Black Expressiveness* (New York: Anchor Press/Doubleday, 1982); J. L. Dillard, *Lexicon of Black English* (New York: Seabury Press, 1977); Henry Louis Gates, Jr., *The Signifying Monkey* (New York: Oxford University Press, 1988); Joseph E. Holloway, ed., *Africanisms in American Culture* (Bloomington: Indiana University Press, 1990).

Clearly, the dozens was widespread in early-twentieth-century Black culture. For example, John Dollard's 1930s research among young Black males in the rural and urban South reports snaps like: "Your ma behind is like a rumble seat. It hang from her back down to her feet," and "Nigger, if I was as ugly as you I would kill myself."[12]

The dozens shows up in popular songs recorded by early bluesmen and -women. In 1929, Speckled Red (Rufus Perryman) made the first recording, which he called "The Dirty Dozen." It became a big hit and was followed by virtually identical recordings by Tampa Red, Leroy Carr, Ben Curry, and other blues artists.[13] World-renowned Leadbelly (Huddie Ledbetter), in his 1935 recording "Kansas City Papa,"[14] incorporated a few lines of the dozens. In the song, the game is played by two women who are "jiving one another." Finally,

11. Gates Thomas, "South Texas Negro Work-Songs," *Publications of the Texas Folklore Society*, No. V (1926). Reference here is from the reprint edition, *Rainbow in the Morning*, ed. J. Frank Dobie (Hatboro, PA: Folklore Associates, Inc., 1965), p. 172.
12. Dollard, "The Dozens: Dialectic of Insult," pp. 7, 11.
13. Paul Oliver, *Aspects of the Blues Tradition* (New York: Oak Publications, 1970), p. 240. In 1956, Speckled Red's famous recording was reissued on an album titled *The Dirty Dozens* for broader distribution. He says he had to "clean it up a bit," but it is so "clean" that it seems like a different song.
14. "Kansas City Papa" can be heard on *Leadbelly: King of the 12-String Guitar*, Sony Music, 1991.

female blues singer Memphis Minnie (Minnie McCoy) showed that women had skills in her 1930 recording "New Dirty Dozen," in which she rocked the house with such lines as:

> I know all about yo pappy and yo mammy,
> Your big fat sister and your little brother Sammy,
> Your aunt and your uncle and your ma's and pa's,
> They all got drunk and showed they Santy Claus.
> Now they all drunken mistreaters, robbers and cheaters
> Slip you in the Dozens, yo poppa is yo cousin
> Yo momma do the Lawdy, Lawd.[15]

Like other games, the dozens has its rules and stock conventions. The simplest form is the verbal retort: "Yo momma," or "Ask yo momma," casually invoked in passing conversation. Check out this recent exchange between two thirty-something Sistas at an exercise spa:

> Linda: Girl, what up with that head? [referring to her friend's hairstyle]
> Betty: Ask yo momma.

Betty's rejoinder can be shrugged off or taken as slipping into the

15. Memphis Minnie, "New Dirty Dozen," 1930, re-released on the album *Blues Classics*, Arhoolie Productions, 1984.

dozens. Linda takes the latter course of action.

> Linda: Oh, so you going there, huh? Well,
> I did ask my momma, and she said,
> "Can't you see that Betty look
> like her momma spit her out?"[16]

Once again, it's on.

Another stock formula, both in the "yo momma" variety and in disses on the person, is the pattern "Yo momma is so *X* that *Y*," or "You are so *X* that *Y*."[17] For example:

> Your mother is so old, she went to the Virgin Mary's baby shower.[18]

> Your mother's teeth are so big, she bit into a sandwich and clipped her toenails.[19]

> Yo momma so slow, it take her an hour to cook Minute Rice, two days to watch *60 Minutes*, and a year to watch *48 Hours*.[20]

16. Recorded by the author in Los Angeles, April 1994, as part of ongoing ethnographic research for *Lyin and Signifyin in the Womanist Text*, work in progress.
17. Linguist William Labov, in an in-depth analysis of the rhetorical complexity of Black insult rituals, concludes that there are at least ten different "shapes" of the "yo momma" disses. See his *Language in the Inner City* (Philadelphia: University of Pennsylvania Press, 1972), pp. 307–321.
18. See page 102, this volume.
19. See page 128, this volume.
20. Recorded by the author on the basketball courts of Lansing, Michigan, May 1992.

The dozens has some fairly sophisticated rules. A fundamental one is that players should be known to each other. Or if not familiar associates, they should at least share membership in and knowledge of the Black cultural context. On this latter point, however, John Baugh contends that the dozens should be restricted to familiar participants because "there is no reliable way to determine the reactions of unfamiliars."[21]

Within the hood, perhaps it would be wise to heed Baugh's advice. Traditionally, males and females only played in same-sex, intimate settings, without outsiders present (or if there were outsiders, the kind who had sense enough not to impose themselves into the game and to follow the cues of the insiders). However, outside the hood, as the game crosses over today, this rule is bending, allowing for public play in front of outsiders and allowing for play by people who may not be intimately known to one another but who are true to the game. Dynamic examples can be heard on television programs like *Def Comedy Jam*, *Martin*, *Living Single,* and *Fresh*

21. John Baugh, *Black Street Speech* (Austin: University of Texas Press, 1983), p. 26.

Prince, and in films like *White Men Can't Jump*.

To be good in the game, your snaps must meet several criteria. First, they must be exaggerated, the wilder, the better, like: "Your mother's mouth is so big, when she inhales, her sneakers get untied."[22] Second, they must employ creative figures of speech, like: "I spoke to your mother today and she said the dentist refuses to give her braces because yellow and silver don't match."[23] Third, the timing of the snap is critical; it must be delivered immediately and spontaneously. This art form is about what rap artists call "freestyling"; it does not allow for lengthy deliberation.

Back in the day, those who aimed for the highest level of mastery of the game insisted on a fourth criterion: rhyming. If you could construct insults that were creatively exaggerated and were expressed in metaphorical language, on time, and with rhyme, you were in the top ten.

22. See page 125, this volume.
23. See page 127, this volume.

Despite the emotionally charged subject matter, snappin works as a game because it is located within the realm of play. Thus the rule that is most crucial to the game is that the snap must not be literally true. For instance, despite all the sexual references in the dozens, nobody has actually gone to bed with anybody's mother. However, if you take snappin out of the realm of play, you enter the real world, where ain nobody playin. Occasionally, though, players will go there, especially when they run out of clever snaps.

As for Black women snappin, the Sistas are on it like a honet, especially when there are no outsiders around. Recently, I asked three professional African American women if they knew how to play the dozens. The women were my middle-aged contemporaries, but I am not part of their intimate circle, and so, as I had anticipated, there was instant denial. I broke the ice by coming out with the opening lines of something called "yo momma's signifyin monkey," which I had heard while hanging out back in the fast days of my youth:

> Down in the jungle where the coconut grows
> Lived yo old-ass momma who was a stomp-down ho.

They laughed, and although one of them continued to deny knowledge of the dozens, after a couple of minutes, all three got all the way up on it.

> Arlene: No, un-unh, I don't think I know any of that stuff.
> Renee: I remember something like, uh, I don't play the dozens cause the dozens is bad—
> Barbara: But, Arlene, I can tell you how many dicks yo' mama had.
> Arlene: Well, I hate to talk about yo momma, Barbara, cause she's a good old soul—
> Renee: Aw, naw, heifer, thought you didn't know any of that stuff.
> Arlene: She got a two-ton pussy and a rubber ass hole.
> Barbara: Hey, wait a minute; that ain't right.[24]

We then got off into a debate about authenticity, Barbara remembering that the phrasing was a "*ten*-ton pussy," and Renee arguing that it was "bad-ass hole." Arlene ended up recounting how, as a teenager, she and her girls would, in effect, call somebody's momma a ho with this snap: "All yo momma's children are step."

In her autobiography, *Gemini*, depicting her childhood in the South, poet Nikki Giovanni, active in the 1960s Black Arts Movement,

24. Recorded by the author in Chicago, March 1994, for *Lyin and Signifyin in the Womanist Text*, work in progress.

relates a story about her sister, Gary, doin the "yo momma" thang. Nikki and Gary were confronted by Peggy and her gang on the streets of Knoxville, Tennessee.

> "Hey, old stuck-up. What you gonna do when your sister's tired of fighting for you?" "I'll beat you up myself. That's what." . . . "You and what army, 'ho'?" "Me and yo' mama's army," Gary answered with precision and dignity. "You talking 'bout my mama?" "I would but the whole town is so I can't add nothing." . . . "You take it back, Gary." Deadly quiet. "Yo' mama's so ugly she went to the zoo and the gorilla paid to see her." "You take that back!" "Yo' mama's such a 'ho' she went to visit a farm and they dug a whole field before they knew it was her."[25]

Then there's presidential inaugural poet Maya Angelou, who is so bad that she once played the *thirteens* in a pair of poems in which she dropped snaps on Blacks and whites to tell each group about their untogetha actions.[26]

The Sistas are deep off into the signifyin dis as well as "yo momma"

25. Nikki Giovanni, *Gemini (An Extended Autobiographical Statement on My First Twenty-five Years of Being a Black Poet)*, first published in 1971 by Bobbs-Merrill. This excerpt is from the Penguin Books edition (New York: Penguin Books, 1976), p. 17.
26. Maya Angelou, *Just Give Me a Cool Drink of Water 'fore I Diiie* (New York: Random House, 1971), pp. 46–47.

snaps. The signifyin is generally delivered with a definite purpose in mind, as was noted by Claudia Mitchell-Kernan in her classic 1960s study of signifyin.[27] Not that Sistas don't have fun with the Word, but the dissin game becomes a vehicle for social commentary. Like the Sista retirees I heard talking about being members of the "packer's club," a snap referring to men who had had so many women in their youth that now, in their mature years, all they could do during sex was "pack chitlins,"[28] i.e., they could not maintain a firm erection. And especially like my girl, Janie, in Zora Neale Hurston's *Their Eyes Were Watching God*. Janie and her husband, Jody, are snappin in front of the group that always hangs out in their store to lie[29] and signify:

> [Jody] A woman stay round uh store till she get old as Methusalem and still can't cut a little thing like a plug of tobacco! Don't stand dere rollin yo pop eyes at me wid yo rump hanging nearly to yo knees!

31

27. Claudia Mitchell-Kernan, "Signifying, Loud-Talking, and Marking," in *Rappin' and Stylin' Out*, ed. Thomas Kochman (Urbana: University of Illinois Press, 1972), pp. 315–35.
28. Smitherman, *Black Talk*, p. 176.
29. A "lie" is an anecdote, experience, reflection, or story, rendered with clever eloquence and oratorical embellishment. Though it may be exaggerated in the telling, the lie has a kernel of truth and is distinguished from an outright falsehood. As Fishbelly asks, in reference to his friend Zeke's having "cut" (had sex with) Laura: "Zeke, this lie about Laura Green . . . is that a *true* lie or just a *plain* old lie?" (From Richard Wright's 1958 novel, *The Long Dream* [New York: Ace Publishing Corporation, 1958], p. 79.)

[Janie] Stop mixin up mah doings wid mah looks, Jody. When you git through tellin me how tuh cut uh plug uh tobacco, then you kin tell me whether mah behind is on straight or not.

[Jody] You must be out yo head . . . talkin any such language as dat.

[Janie] You de one started talkin under people's clothes. Not me.

[Jody] Whut's de matter wid you, nohow? You ain't no young girl to be gettin all insulted bout yo looks. You ain't no young courtin' gal. You'se uh ole woman, nearly forty.

[Janie] Yeah, ah'm nearly forty and you'se already fifty. . . . Talkin bout *me* lookin old! When you pull down yo britches, you look lak de change uh life.[30]

Like I said, the Sistas be all over signifyin. Excellent examples in the 1990s are the women's "war council" in Spike Lee's film *Jungle Fever* and the birthday celebration in Terry McMillan's novel *Waiting to Exhale.*

Today's snaps seem less reliant on the standard formulas and stock phrases that characterized old-school snaps. You don't hear too much of the "I hate to talk bout yo momma/She's a good old soul" rhyming style of the dozens. Still it's obvious that 1990s snaps are grounded in the African American Oral Tradition.

30. Hurston, *Their Eyes Were Watching God*, pp. 74–75.

As a linguist with an unabashed love and respect for the power of language, I can't wait to see how future generations will stamp their imprint upon the game. Like, don't you think that it would be fascinating to hear the snaps of, say, a hundred years from now? I'll be there to write about it. If I'm lyin, I'm flyin.

—GENEVA SMITHERMAN, PH.D.

UNIVERSITY DISTINGUISHED PROFESSOR OF ENGLISH

DIRECTOR, AFRICAN AMERICAN LANGUAGE AND LITERACY PROGRAM,

MICHIGAN STATE UNIVERSITY

AUTHOR OF *BLACK TALK: WORDS AND PHRASES FROM THE HOOD TO THE AMEN CORNER*

FAT
SNAPS

Your mother has so many rings around her belly, she has to screw on her underwear.

Your father is so fat, you have to MEASURE HIS WAIST with first-down markers.

Your mother is so fat, Richard Simmons won't deal her a meal.

Your mother is so fat, you could slap her leg and RIDE THE WAVES.

Your mother is so fat, she wakes up in sections.

Your butt is so big, if you farted today it wouldn't come out till next week. —ARDIE

Your mother's thighs are so big, when they rub they talk to each other: "You let me go by and I'll let you go by."

Your mother is so fat, she drives a spandex car.

You're so fat, you have to travel on THE GRAVY TRAIN.

Your mother is so fat, her measurements are 36-24-36 and her other arm is just as big. —FIG

Your mother is so fat, she uses the highway for a Slip 'N Slide.

Your mother is so fat, when she steps on the railroad tracks the crossing lights come on.

Your mother is so fat, WHEN SHE TAKES OFF HER DRAWERS they start to pant.

Your mother is so fat, she could sell shade.

Your mother is so fat, when she goes to the beach kids yell, "Free Willy! Free Willy!" —A. G. WHITE

You're so fat, it looks like you've got a hangover because your stomach's always hanging over your belt.

Your mother is so fat, in a WHITE T-SHIRT she looks like a garbage truck.

You're so fat, it takes an hour to wash each butt cheek. —MUGGA

YOU'RE SO FAT, when you took your suit to the cleaners they said, "We don't clean parachutes."

Your mother is so fat, she puts mayonnaise on aspirin.

You're so fat, I saw a picture of you as a kid and you were stuck in a Hula-Hoop. —DR. DRE, HOT 97

Your sister is so fat, when she walks it looks like she's smuggling Volkswagens. —FROM *IN LIVING COLOR*

Your mother is so fat, she can do the wave by herself.

Your sister is so fat, her picture weighs ten pounds.

Your mother is so fat, **AFTER A SHOWER** she dries herself with a squeegee.

You're so fat, if cellulite were a penny a pound you'd be a millionaire.

Your mother is so fat, **SHE SAT ON A RAINBOW** and made Skittles. —FROM *SISTER ACT II*

Your sister is so fat, she was lying on a beach and some dude named Raoul came up, stuck a flag in her ass, and claimed her for Spain.

Your mother is so fat, she has back-up lights.

Your mother is so fat, she eats biscuits like Tic Tacs.

—FROM *IN LIVING COLOR*

Your mother is so fat, she got on a scale and it said, "One at a time, please."

Your mother is so fat, she got hit by a bus and said, "WHO THREW THE ROCK?"

Your mother is so fat, every time she puts on a yellow dress people yell, "Taxi!"

Your mother is so fat, she lives in TWO ZIP CODES.

Your mother is so fat, she has to take a shit in the bathtub.

Your father is so fat, when he walks down the street he makes POTHOLES.

Your mother is so fat, she was lying on the beach and Greenpeace rolled her back into the ocean.

Your mother is so fat, if she wore a green and white sweater she'd look like A FOOTBALL FIELD. —ROB MAGNOTTI

Your sister is so fat, she doesn't take pictures, she takes posters.

Your mother is so fat, she can't lose weight, she can only find it.

YOUR SISTER IS SO FAT, SHE USES A MATTRESS FOR A MAX

Your sister is so fat, they had to let out her car seats.

Your mother is so fat, she has more nooks and crannies than AN ENGLISH MUFFIN. —ROB MAGNOTTI

Your mother is so fat, she uses a blanket as a washcloth.

45

Your mother is so fat, when she sleeps she gets stuck in her dreams.

Your sister is so fat, when she steps on a boat it becomes a submarine.

Your mother is so fat, she tried to WATCH HER WEIGHT and got two black eyes.

Your mother is so fat, she uses Greyhound buses for Rollerblades.

Your sister is so fat, they call her Mack because she's built like a truck.

Your mother is so fat, she carries A TELEPHONE BOOTH for a cellular phone.

Your sister is so fat, she wipes her ass with a mattress.

Your mother is so fat, she uses a parachute for a shower cap.

Your father is so fat, he has more rolls THAN A BREAD SHOP.

Your mother is so fat, Weight Watchers can't stand to look at her.

You're so fat, when you were a baby you didn't have a baby carriage, you had a shopping cart.

Your sister is so fat, SHE WEARS A HULA-HOOP for a pinkie ring.

Your brother is so fat, he has to shower at the car wash.

Your mother is so fat, every time she tries to get out of bed she ROCKS HERSELF back to sleep.

You're so fat, when you were missing they couldn't fit your picture on a milk carton—they had to put it on a milk truck.

Your brother is so fat, they call him Astronaut because he just takes up space.

Your mother is so fat, she uses a water cooler to douche.

YOU'RE SO FAT, YOUR LEVI'S AREN'T 501S— THEY'RE 747s.

STUPID
SNAPS

Your mother is so dumb, she thinks the Last Supper is when your family runs out of food stamps.

Your mother is so stupid, she thought MENOPAUSE was a button on a tape deck.

Your mother is so stupid, she put her son in rehab because he was HOOKED ON PHONICS.

You're so dumb, you went to the zoo to buy Christmas seals.

Your mother is so stupid, she put water on her chest for heartburn.

Your mother is so stupid, I told her to go downtown, so she started eating HER OWN PUSSY. —TERRY HODGES

If brains were lard, you couldn't grease a skillet.

—JED CLAMPETT, *THE BEVERLY HILLBILLIES*

Your father is so dumb, he stole a car and kept up the payments.

—BROOKLYN MIKE

Your brother is so dumb, he asked me how to spell AT&T.

Your sister is so dumb, she's the poster child for stupidity.

Your mother is so dumb, she went to the post office for food stamps. —BROOKLYN MIKE

Your mother is so dumb, she saw the YMCA and said, "Look, they misspelled 'Macys!' "

Your father is so stupid, he saw a sign that said "Wet Floor," SO HE TOOK A PISS.

Your father is so stupid, I told him to chill and he got into the freezer.

Your mother is so dumb, she has high-heel slippers. —TRACY MORGAN

Your little brother is so stupid, he ties his laces with spaghetti so he can eat and run.

You're so dumb, you need a tutor to **TIE YOUR TIMBERLANDS.** —MACIO

You're so dumb, you put a phone receiver up your butt waiting for a "booty call." —UNCLE JIMMY MACK

YOUR SO STUPID, A BAND ON HER

Your sister is so dumb, she robbed a bank and hid in a police car.

—BROOKLYN MIKE

Your father is a dumb Mississippi pimp, always talking about "Bitch better have my sweet potatoes."

Your mother is so stupid, I told her to speak up and she started **YELLING AT THE SKY.**

55

Your mother is so dumb, she got fired from a blow job.

—C. J. MORGAN, WQUE

Your mother is so stupid, she thinks the INSTITUTION OF MARRIAGE is a college.

You're so dumb, you think soul food is dinner for one.

Your mother is so dumb, she thinks EX-LAX IS A MUSLIM.

—JERRY KUPFER

You're so dumb, you think babies can be found in the infantry.

Your mother's so dumb, she almost strangled herself with A CORDLESS PHONE.

You're so stupid, if you gave me a penny for your thoughts you'd have change coming back. —FROM *IN LIVING COLOR*

Your brother is so dumb, I yelled "Duck!" during a shoot-out and he screamed, "Quack, Quack!"

You're so dumb, you need directions to use TOILET PAPER.

Your mother is so dumb, she sold the car for gas money.

Your sister is so dumb, she went to a Chinese restaurant for an ORDER OF PROTECTION.

Your mother's so dumb, when she asked me what letter comes after *X* I said, "*Y*," and she said, "'cause I want to know." —TALENT

YOUR MOTHER'S SO STUPID, she thinks the board of education is a piece of lumber.

Your mother is so dumb, she tried to change the channel on a TV dinner.

Your mother is so dull, she could make the lights DIM.

YOUR FATHER IS SO STUPID, HE GOT FIRED FROM THE M&M FACTORY FOR THROWING AWAY Ws.

I was going to get a brain like yours, BUT MY PENNY GOT STUCK in the machine.

Your mom is so stupid, I told her to take the number 4 bus, so she took the number 2 bus twice.

Your sister is so dumb, on her birthday she lit a match to see if she blew out all the candles. —TRACY MORGAN

Your mother is so dumb, she thought MCI was a rapper.

Your brother is so dumb, he got his dick stuck in button-fly jeans.

Your mother is so dumb, every time she's at a traffic light that says "Don't Walk," she runs.

Your mother is so dumb, she brought a spoon to the Super Bowl.

Your sister is so dumb, on a job application where it asks who to contact in case of an emergency, she put "911." —BROOKLYN MIKE

You're so dumb, on the way to the airport YOU SAW A SIGN that said "Airport Left," so you went home.

Your sister is so dumb, she spells farm *E-I-E-I-O*. —TRACY MORGAN

Your mother is so dumb, she brought a ladder to a Giants game.

—TRACY MORGAN

Your mother is so stupid, she stood up on an EMPTY BUS.

Your mother is so dumb, she lost her unemployment because of a blow job.

Your mother is so dumb, she needs a recipe for ice cubes.

Your mother is so dumb, SHE BOILS HER NIPPLES before breast-feeding.

Your sister is so dumb, she puts a condom on her vibrator.

Your brother is so dumb, he has a kickstand on his tricycle.

Your mother is so dumb, her job was sleeping and she got fired
FOR WAKING UP.

Your father is so stupid, he lost his job as an elevator operator
because he forgot the route.

You're so dumb, when you were born your mother should have been
arrested for smuggling dope.

Your father is so dumb, he keeps underwear in his briefcase.

Your father's so stupid, when he hears a snowblower he pulls his pants down. —HOWARD STERN, WXRK

You're so dumb, you tried to wake up a sleeping bag.

Your mother is so stupid, she thought CHICKEN POT PIE was a fraternity.

Your mother is so dumb, I asked for crackers in my soup and she went and got four white guys.

YOUR FATHER IS SO DUMB, HE WAS **DRIVING** AND SAW A SIGN THAT SAID **DRAW BRIDGE,** SO HE PULLED OUT A PAD AND **PENCIL.**

Your mother is so dumb, she took the Pepsi challenge AND CHOSE JIF. —TRACY MORGAN

Your sister is so stupid, she walked into a Store 24 and asked what time they close.

You're so dumb, you get lost riding an elevator.

Your brother is so dumb, he tries to do wheelies on a unicycle.

Your mom is so dumb, she climbed A GLASS WALL to see what was on the other side.

Your mom is so dumb, she took toilet paper to a crap game.

Your mother is DUMB AND DYSLEXIC, she thought an IUD was the charge for drunk driving.

Your mother is so stupid, she went to Dr. Dre for a pap smear.
—FROM IN LIVING COLOR

Your mother is so stupid, she thinks a Moon Pie is an ass WITH WHIPPED CREAM. —FROM IN LIVING COLOR

Your mother is so stupid, she went to White Castle to see royalty.

YOU'RE SO DUMB, YOU HAVE TO GO TO THE CELLAR FOR A DEEP

Your brother is so dumb, he has a leg on the side of his head and is waiting for his brain to kick in. —TALENT

Your sister is so dumb, she thinks eyeball is a sport.

Your father is so dumb, he thought *TIME MAGAZINE* was something that inmates read.

Your father is so dumb, he brought his fishing rod to a car pool.

THOUGHT.

Your mother is so dumb, she thought Timex was a Muslim watch company.

Your mother's so stupid, when I told her to SQUEAL LIKE A PIG she said, "Mooo." —FROM *IN LIVING COLOR*

Your mother is so dumb, she asked me what "yield" means and I said, "Go slow." She said, "Whaaaaaaaaat doeeeeeeeeeeees yieeeeeeeeeld meeeeeeeeeeean?"

Your mother is so stupid, she failed a urine test.

Your mother is so dumb, she thinks a dustpan is something YOU COOK DIRT IN.

UGLY
SNAPS

If ugliness were an album, you'd go platinum.

Your mother is so ugly, they chopped down her family tree and BURNED IT.

Your mother is so ugly, I took her to the zoo and the zookeeper said, "Thanks for bringing her back." —CHUCK NICE

Your mother is so ugly, her baby pictures show the BACK OF HER HEAD.

Your mother is so ugly, she had to get the baby drunk to breast-feed it.

Your mother is so ugly, she went to see a freak show and got offered a permanent job.

You're so ugly, your parents rent out your baby videos for horror films.

Your sister is so ugly, MEN HANG UP ON HER when they call for phone sex.

Your mother is so ugly, police artists are afraid to sketch her.

Your mother is so ugly, you tell people you were adopted.

YOUR MOTHER IS SO UGLY, WHEN SHE SWIMS IT LOOKS LIKE THE BAY OF PIGS.

Your mother is so ugly, she has to use ALUMINUM FOIL for a mirror.

Your sister is so ugly, when she got sick they called a vet.

Your mother is so ugly, she makes blind kids cry.

Your father is so ugly, farmers USE HIS PICTURE for a scarecrow.

Your girlfriend is so ugly, every time she goes outside she gets chased by the dogcatcher.

You're so ugly, WHEN YOU JERK OFF your hand tries to go to sleep.

Your mother is so ugly, she swam in the Mississippi and they skimmed ugly for six months.

—ALAN LOMAX, *THE LAND WHERE THE BLUES BEGAN*

You're so ugly, you have to sneak up on the dark.

Your skin is so bumpy, a blind man could read your face.

Your sister is so ugly, I paid her to HAUNT A HOUSE.

I hear your girlfriend comes from a mixed background, half pit bull, half rottweiler.

Your mother is so ugly, she could turn Barry *White* into Al *Green*.

You're so ugly, the last time I saw something like you I flushed it DOWN THE DRAIN.

You're so ugly, you can't hail a bus.

Your mother is so ugly, her nickname should be Moses 'cause every time she steps in water it parts.

Your mother is so ugly, she had to find A BEAUTICIAN that makes house calls.

Your mom is so ugly, she gives Freddy Krueger nightmares.

Your mother's so ugly, people put pictures of her in their car windows to keep their radios from getting stolen.

You're so ugly, they let you park in handicapped spaces.

You're so ugly, when you threw a boomerang IT DIDN'T COME BACK.

Your father's so ugly, when I took him to the zoo he needed two tickets, one to get in and one to get out.

You're so ugly, you can't get a date off a calendar.

If ugliness were music, your mother would be an 8-track. —MACIO

Your sister is so ugly, I heard they had to rush her to the beauty parlor IN AN AMBULANCE.

You were such an ugly baby, the doctor had to spank you with his eyes closed.

You were such an ugly baby, when you were born your mom got fined for illegal dumping.

You were such an ugly baby, when your mother went into labor THE DOCTORS WENT ON STRIKE.

You're so ugly, your last name is Link and your first name is Missing.

Your girlfriend is so ugly, OPP means "Oh, please, put it away."

Your mother is so ugly, she could look up A CAMEL'S ASS and scare the hump off his back.

Your mom is so ugly, when I took her to the pet shop they put her in the window.

Your mother is so ugly, I took her to a dude ranch and a horse said, "Are you my relief?"

You're so ugly, in your family photo album they only keep THE NEGATIVES. —XAVIER CADEAU

BIG
AND
SMALL
SNAPS

Your butt is so big, when you back up you beep.

Your ears are so big, it looks like two men jumped out of a cab and LEFT THE DOORS OPEN.

Your lips are so big, you don't use Chap Stick, you use Mop & Glo.

Your dick is so small, you bought it a *condominium*.

—ROB BARTLETT ON WFAN *IMUS IN THE MORNING*

Your dick is SO SMALL, when your girl sucks it she looks like she's smoking a roach.

Your tits are so big, your nickname is "Moo."

Your mother is so small, she's only got ONE FLOWER on her print panties.

Your mother's tits are so big, when you put your ear to her chest you can hear the ocean. —TONY WOODS

Your sister's tits are so small, she could use a Band-Aid for a bra.

Your mother's head is so big, when she passed a satellite dish store, she asked, "Are those hats on sale?"

YOUR SISTER'S BUTT IS SO BIG, SHE WEARS A LICENSE PLATE ON HER ASS.

Your mother's lips are so big, she uses roll-on deodorant for lipstick.

Your mom is so big, she shoots marbles with bowling balls.

Your nose is so big, when you breathe you INHALE THE CURTAINS.

Your lips are so big, you could pull them over your head and wear them as a beanie. —TISHA CAMPBELL, ON MARTIN

Your girlfriend's ass is so small, I've seen bigger butts on a cigarette.

Your lips are so big, you need a hat so pigeons don't shit on them.

Your lips are so big, your car doesn't need AIR BAGS.

Your car is so small, the radio is in the backseat.

Your mother's ears are so big, she can hear the clouds.

Your mother is so big, she was standing on the corner and the police said, "HEY, BREAK IT UP!"

HAIR
SNAPS

YOUR HAIR WEAVE is so long, it's got more extensions than AT&T. —FIG

Your mother's hair is so short, she needs Velcro braids.

Your mother is so hairy, you could sell her as a Chia Pet.

YOUR FATHER IS SO BALD, he looks like a tall testicle.

Your father is so bald, if he put on a turtleneck he'd look like a busted condom. —FROM *IN LIVING COLOR*

Your mother is so bald, she wears a wig with a chin strap.

YOUR FATHER IS SO BALD, he has holes in his pockets so he can run his fingers through his hair.

Your mother is so hairy, she has to part the hair on her ass just to take a shit.

Your mother is so bald, her head looks like **A SPLIT PEA.**

Your nose is so hairy, it looks like you've got Afros growing out your nostrils.

MOTHER'S HAIR IS

Your hair is so long, **IT'S UNBEWEAVABLE.** —FIG

NAPPY,

Your mother is so bald, you can see what she's thinking.
—FROM *IN LIVING COLOR*

IT HER

BLEED.

SMELLY

SNAPS

Your mother's breath is so bad, the ice-cream man gave her a Listerine Popsicle.

Your sister's drawers are so smelly, she uses Odor-Eaters for panty shields. —FROM *IN LIVING COLOR*

Your breath is so stank, I don't know whether you need gum or toilet paper.

Your mother's breath is so bad, skunks say, "HI, MOM."

Your mother's breath is so bad, she sucks on Odor-Eaters.

YOUR GIRLFRIEND'S BREATH IS SO BAD, FOUR OUT OF FIVE DENTISTS RECOMMEND SHE GARGLE WITH SUMMER'S EVE.

Your mother stinks so bad, she sweats BLACK FLAG.

Your sister's breath is so bad, whenever she opens her mouth she's talkin' shit.

Your mother smells so bad, bloodhounds won't chase her.

You smell so bad, you make Right Guard turn left . . . you make Secret obvious . . . you make Speed Stick slow down . . . and you get Sure confused. —A. G. WHITE

YOUR BREATH IS SO HOT, it boils water.

HOUSE
SNAPS

Your house is so small, the welcome mat just says WEL.

—JOE CLAIRE

Your house is so small, if you dropped a washcloth it would look like wall-to-wall carpeting. —MICHAEL EPPS

Your house is so small, when I rang the doorbell the toilet flushed.

Your house is so small, I opened the front door and stepped into THE BACKYARD.

You got so many roaches in your house, you made them sign a lease.

Your house is so small, we had to eat a Bigfoot pizza outside.

—A. G. WHITE

Your house is so dirty, I slipped on a rat and a roach stole my wallet.

Your house is so small, THE FRONT AND BACK DOOR are on the same hinge.

Your house is so nasty, you have mousetraps in the icebox.

Your hometown is so small, the Greyhound buses have puppies on the side.

YOUR HOUSE IS SO NASTY, THE ROACHES WEAR SLIPPERS.

Your house is so dirty, the cockroaches use 4 x 4s to cross the kitchen floor.

Your house is so dirty, when I tried to kill a cockroach it said, "STOP, WE'RE FAMILY."

The dust is so thick in your house, the roaches wear snowshoes.
—ED LOVER, HOT 97

OLD
SNAPS

Your mother is so old, she gave dinosaurs head. —RONDA FOWLER

Your mother is so old, she went to the VIRGIN MARY'S baby shower.

Your mother is so old, she got baptized in sand.

Your mother is so old, she used to drive chariots to high school. —FROM *WHITE MEN CAN'T JUMP*

Your mom is so old, when God said, "Let there be light," she flipped the switch. —GEORGE WALLACE

Your mother is so old, she knew the Great Wall when it was just OKAY.

Your mother is so old, she's in Jesus's yearbook.

Your mother is so old, her birthday fell off the calendar.

Your mother's neck is so wrinkled, she could GRATE CHEESE. —ROB BARTLETT ON WFAN *IMUS IN THE MORNING*

Your mother is so old, I broke into a pyramid and saw a picture of her with King Tut in a headlock.

Your mother is so old, she squeaks. —PATRICK ELLIS, WHUR

Your mother's tits are so saggy, she got stopped in a 7-Eleven for **STEALING PIES** under her shirt.

Your mother is so old, she saw Jesus walking on water and said, "It's gotta be the shoes!" —TALENT

Your mother's ass is like an old Run DMC movie, it's tougher than leather. —MACIO

Your mother is so old, **SHE BLEEDS DUST.**

Your mother is so old, she has a Jesus Christ Starter jacket.
—MICHAEL BLACKSON

Your mother is so old, she was *two* when the West was *won*.

Your mother is so old, she went to retire at **JURASSIC PARK.**—YOLANDA CARMICHAEL-WHITE, WIZF

Your mother is so old, she knew Cap'n Crunch when he was just a sailor.

Your mother is so old, she needs a belt to hold her skin up. —TALENT

Your mother is so old, she was on the guest list for Noah's ark.

Your mother is so old, she used to baby-sit God.

Your mother is so old, she took her driving test on a dinosaur.

Your mother is so old, she CARRIES GROCERIES in the bags under her eyes.

POOR
SNAPS

Your family is so poor, they think MATCHED LUGGAGE is two shopping bags from the same store.

You're so po', you can't afford the *o* and *r*.

Your family is so poor, your father eats his cereal with a fork so he can pass the milk around the table. —BERNIE MAC

Your mother is so poor, I saw her pitching pennies in the gutter and asked what she was doing, she said, "Paying the rent."

Your family is so poor, they have to put Kool-Aid on layaway.

Your family is so poor, your father was voted un-employee of the month.

Your mother is SO COUNTRY, she had corn bread for her wedding cake.

Your father is so poor, he got a part-time job painting Skittles.
—TRACY MORGAN

You're so poor, your FOOD STAMPS bounced.

Your family is so poor, salt and pepper aren't seasonings, they're the main course.

Your family is so poor, they think going through clear garbage bags is WINDOW-SHOPPING.

Your family has been on welfare so long, your mother thinks WIC means "Welfare is cool." —ARDIE

Your family is so poor, either they eat oatmeal or they eat no meal. —BERNIE MAC

You're so poor, you lick stamps FOR DINNER.

You're so poor, you have a pet roach. —FAT JOE THE GANGSTER

Your family is so poor, when you broke your arm they sent you to THE AIRPORT for an X ray.

Your family is so poor, I saw your father crawling in a cardboard box yelling, "I'm home."

Your family is so poor, when they bought you a three-piece suit, you wore the jacket, your sister wore the vest, and your brother wore the pants. —BERNIE MAC

You're so poor, your car doesn't have an air bag, just a steering wheel with a pillow. —MICHAEL EPPS

Your mother is so poor, she's got a wig with bald spots.

NASTY

SNAPS

Your sister is so nasty, she has more clap than an auditorium.

Your sister is so nasty, I called her ON THE PHONE and got an ear infection.

Your mom is so nasty, she worked at a sperm bank and got fired for drinking on the job. —MONIQUE WATKINS

Your underwear has so many streaks, you could use it as a road map.

Your mother is so nasty, she wears long dresses to hide the NO-PEST STRIP. —HOWARD STERN, WXRK

Your mother is so sweaty, Nike named a sweatband after her.

—PATRICK EWING, NEW YORK KNICKS

Your girlfriend is so nasty, her gynecologist examines her with a telescope.

Your mother is so nasty, there's a sign by her pussy that reads MAY CAUSE IRRITATION AND DROWSINESS.

Your sister is so nasty, she has sourdough yeast infections.

Your sister is so nasty, crabs bungee-jump off her tampon strings.

Your feet are so crusty, I thought you were making A PIE.

Your mother is so religious, she always says grace before picking her nose. —HOWARD STERN, WXRK

Your mother is so greasy, she sweats Crisco.

Your brother is so dirty, he has to WIPE HIS FEET to play in the dirt.

Your mother is so nasty, when I asked her what was for dinner she put her foot on the plate and said, "Corn."

Your mother is so nasty, I can tell when she's having her period 'cause she's only wearing one sock. —HOWARD STERN, WXRK

Your mother is so nasty, when I drove her home I said I needed gas in my car, **SO SHE FARTED.** —MACIO

Your feet have so many corns, if you added some lima beans you'd have succotash.

Your father's feet are so hard and crusty, when he walks across the floor it sounds like he's tap dancing. —CEDRIC THE ENTERTAINER

Your mother is so nasty, men can't eat her pussy without a lifeguard **ON DUTY**.

Your mother is like the Boston Celtics, she only showers after the fourth period.

Your mother is so nasty, she buys her panties from Petland Discounts.

Your mother is so nasty, she likes ORAL SEX for the view.

Your father's feet have more crust than Kentucky Fried Chicken.
—ROB MAGNOTTI

Your mother is so nasty, when someone said, "Hit the dirt," I jumped on her back.

You're so nasty, you use your earwax on your car. —MUGGA

Your mother is so nasty, after a bath she leaves a ring around the tub—and a BRACELET.

Your mother is so nasty, when she takes off her panties it sounds like Velcro.

Your mother's tits are so nasty, when she danced topless a CHEESE LINE formed outside.

SHORT
SNAPS

You're so short, when you sit on the curb your feet dangle.

Your mother is so short, she could pose FOR TROPHIES.

—JAMIE FOX ON *IN LIVING COLOR*

Your mother is so short, firemen keep attaching hoses to her tits.

—ROB BARTLETT ON WFAN *IMUS IN THE MORNING*

Your mother is so short, she could choke lacing up high-tops.

Your mother is so short, when she blushes she looks LIKE A MATCHSTICK.

YOUR FATHER IS SO SHORT, HE'S A BOUNCER AT A ROACH MOTEL.

YOUR MOTHER IS SO SHORT, she could do the limbo under a spoon.

Your mother is so short, she needs a ladder to suck an ant's dick.

Your mother is so short, she had kids so she'd have someone to look up to.

Your mother is so short, she thinks AN ICE CUBE IS A GLACIER.

You're so short, you tripped on spit. —FAT JOE THE GANGSTER

TEETH

AND

MOUTH

SNAPS

Your mouth is so rotten, you have a sign on your gums "Next Tooth 3 Miles."

Your teeth are so big, it looks like you have BABY SHOES in your mouth.

Your teeth are so yellow, when you close your mouth your stomach lights up. —TERRY HODGES

You're missing so many teeth, it looks like your tongue's in jail.

Your mouth is so big, when you inhale, your sneakers get untied.

YOUR MOTHER'S TEETH ARE SO YELLOW, WHEN SHE SMILES CARS YIELD.

Your sister's teeth are so crooked, Amtrak had to install her braces.

Your teeth are SO ROTTEN, when you smile it looks like you've got dice in your mouth.

Your teeth are so yellow, the dentist won't give you braces 'cause yellow and silver don't match. —MACIO

Your breath is so bad, the dentist TAKES ANESTHETIC before filling your cavities.

Your mother's gums are so black, she spits Yoo-hoo.

Your mother's teeth are so big, she bit into a sandwich and clipped her toenails.

Your mother's mouth is so nasty, she has to brush her teeth with hair remover.

Your brother has ONE TOOTH and they call him Chopper One.

Your mom's teeth are so gapped, she picks them with baseball bats.

Your teeth are so big, you floss with a jump rope.

SKINNY

SNAPS

Your mother is so skinny, she could shit through a straw.

Your mother is so skinny, she can walk through the EYE OF A NEEDLE.

You're so skinny, you could use a condom for a sleeping bag.

Your brother is so skinny, if he had dreadlocks I could hold him upside down and mop the floor.

Your girlfriend is so skinny, when she stands by your car she looks like THE ANTENNA.

YOUR FATHER IS SO SKINNY, EVERY TIME HE FARTS HIS BACK GOES OUT.

Your sister is so skinny, HER BRA FITS BETTER backward.

Your mother is so skinny, she has to rent a shadow.

Your mother is so skinny, if she stuck a piece of rice down her throat she'd look like a hanger.

Your dad is so skinny, he can do push-ups under the door.

Your mother is so skinny, she swallowed a marble and looked like she was pregnant. —JAMIE FOX ON IN LIVING COLOR

You're so skinny, if you put a dime on your head you'd look like a nail.

You're so skinny, when you walk down the street you fall through THE GRATES.

Your mother's butt is so flat, I had to flip her with a spatula.

Your family is so skinny, if they CARRIED A CANOE they'd look like a comb.

Your sister is so flat, I've got mosquito bites bigger than her tits.

YOUR FATHER IS SO SKINNY, HE COULD GET A JOB AS A PINSTRIPE ON A SUIT.

Your mother is so skinny, she could win the MISS SOMALIA pageant.

You're so skinny, when you turn sideways you disappear.

Your mother is so skinny, she uses CHAP STICK for roll-on deodorant.

You're so skinny, you can't take a shower because you keep slipping down the drain.

You're so skinny, a snowflake can knock you over.

EYE

SNAPS

Your mother is so cross-eyed, she complains she can't cross the street because one light is ALWAYS RED.

Your mother's glasses are so thick, she can stare into space and see astronauts waving at her.

Your mother's eyes are so red, when she stands on a corner cars stop.

Your mother is SO CROSS-EYED, she went to a movie and thought it was a double feature.

Your mother is so cross-eyed, she has to take off her Walkman to see.

Your mother is so cross-eyed, she dropped a dime and picked up two nickels. —MICHAEL EPPS

Your glasses are **SO THICK,** they look like a check-cashing window. —MACIO

You're so blind, the windows in your house are prescription.

Your mother's glasses are so thick, when she looks up at the sun her eyelashes catch on fire.

Your glasses are so thick, you can see the future.

MOTHER IS SO

Your mother is so cross-eyed, when she goes to the movies she has to sit sideways.

-EYED,

Your mother is so cross-eyed, she can watch a tennis match just by **STARING AT THE NET.**

ONLY CHILD

Your glasses are so thick, they have a warning on them: "Objects May Be Closer Than They Appear."

TWIN.

BODY
SNAPS

Your mother's got a wooden leg with a KICKSTAND.

—EDDIE MURPHY IN *DELIRIOUS*

Your mother's got no fingers and tried to press charges.

Your mother's got one ear and wants to hear both sides of the story.

Your mother has no arms and tried to throw a block party.

Your mother has ONE LEG LONGER than the other and they call her Hip-Hop. —ROB STAPLETON

Your mother has no fingers and she wants to be down with the POINTER SISTERS.

Your mother has got one leg and bought a pair of New Balance sneakers.

COLOR
SNAPS

Your family is so black, IF THEY HELD HANDS they'd look like a stretch limo.

You're so white, you think Malcolm X's name is Malcolm the Tenth.

Your mother is so black, the sun sends her bills.

Your father is so black, when he gets in a car THE OIL LIGHT turns on.

Your mother is so black, when she sits in a Jacuzzi she turns the water to hot chocolate.

You're so black, you cast a shadow on coal.

Your mother is so black, when she goes out in daylight the street-lights come on.

Your mother is so black, IF YOU BOTTLED HER she'd look like soy sauce.

Your father is so black, he needs a license to drink white milk.

Your mother is so black, she put lotion on her legs and it looked like she was wearing leather pants.

Your family is so black, when they walk at night they disappear.

Your mother is SO ASHY, if she walked into a classroom naked she'd be a chalkboard.

Your mother is so black, she got a part-time job as midnight.

Your mother is so black, IF SHE JUMPED IN THE OCEAN it would be an oil spill.

Your mom is so black, she could leave a fingerprint on charcoal.
—BERNIE MAC

Your father is so black, HE PISSES OIL.

Your sister is so black, lightning bugs follow her in the daytime.

SEX
SNAPS

148

Your mother's like a bag of chips, she's FREE-TO-LAY.

—MACIO

Your sister is like a bowling ball, she gets picked up, fingered, thrown in the gutter, and still comes back for more. —ARDIE

Your mother's so horny, her vibrator comes with jumper cables.

You're so horny, you'd fuck the crack of dawn.

Your father is like a Mounds bar, HE'S GOT NO NUTS.

—ROB MAGNOTTI

Your mother's like THE COMMODORES, she's easy like Sunday morning. —MACIO

Your mother is like the Pillsbury Doughboy, everybody gets a poke.

Your mother is like a hardware store, she gets lots of screws.

Your father's such a pedophile, his bumper sticker says HAVE I HUGGED YOUR KID TODAY? —HOWARD STERN, WXRK

Your mother is so loose, the only reason she wears panties is to keep her ankles warm.

Your sister is like a lollipop, ten cents a lick.

YOUR FATHER'S SO HORNY, he's seen more tail than a veterinarian.

Your mother's like a fancy restaurant—both take deliveries in the rear. —HOWARD STERN, WXRK

You're so gay, when you sleep they call you Fruit Roll-up.

Your dick is so small, when you get a blow job it looks like a Tic Tac in the mouth of a whale. —ADELE GIVENS

YOUR SISTER IS SO LOOSE, SHE CAN GOLF SUCK A BALL THROUGH A GARDEN HOSE.

Your mother is like a birthday cake, everyone gets a blow.

Your sister sucks so much dick, her lips went platinum.

Your mother is so loud during sex, when she finishes, the neighbors have a cigarette. —JANICE YOUNG

YOUR GIRL IS SO LOOSE, she sucks dick just to keep her face warm.

Your sister is so loose, she sat on a bar stool and fell all the way to the floor.

Your mother is so loose, they call her Computer 'cause she's every-body's laptop. —HOWARD STERN, WXRK

Your sister's pubic hair is SO NAPPY, the crabs drive around in dune buggies.

Your mother is so horny, her vibrator has dual exhaust.

I wouldn't say your father's gay, but I don't think Lisa is his real name. —TRACY MORGAN

Your mother is like a squirrel, she always has a nut in her mouth.

YOUR MOTHER'S PUSSY IS SO DRY, THE CRABS CARRY CANTEENS.

Your sister is so loose, she's got "Over One Billion Served" tattooed between her legs.

Your sister is like a buffet—everyone can help themselves.

Your mother is so loose, they call her Microwave 'cause she gets hot in fifteen seconds. —HOWARD STERN, WXRK

Your mother's legs are like PEANUT BUTTER, smooth and easy to spread.

Your sister is so loose, she has a sex menu tattooed on her back.

Your mother is so horny, SHE GOES TO CHURCH just to play with the organ.

Your mother's pussy is so big, when your father puts it in he says, "Baby, it's cold outside." —DR. DRE, HOT 97

YOUR SISTER'S LEGS are like 7-Eleven, open twenty-four hours a day.

Your sister is like a refrigerator, everyone sticks their meat inside.

MOVES
AND
STANCES
FOR ADVANCED
SNAPPING

DON'T GO THERE

A defensive move to thwart an incoming snap. Also a warning that you are entering a dangerous subject.

LONG DIS

Created by hecklers to express disapproval of a performer onstage.

FLAT LINE
Indicates a dead snap.

ONE-FINGER HOOK
Used to add emphasis when landing a snap.

TWO-FINGER HOOK

Same as One-Finger Hook, but with two fingers.

HEAD TO HEAD

This advanced move is used to escalate a battle. Bad breath helps here.

STANDING 8

A forced smile by an embattled snapper to show he can go on *fighting.*

STARE DOWN

This is as close as snappers can come to physical intimidation without actually making contact. Lead with your chest and keep eye contact.

THE ROLL

Rolling your eyes upward to indicate
a whack snap.

SNAP ATTACK

Snapping on your opponent from
behind. Only to be used when the
audience or crowd is in front of the
battle, as opposed to a "battle in
the round."

MAIL BAG

I thought your book was something that needed to be written. Not just because of the fact that you compiled a bunch of bags and put them in a book, but because you gave information on their history as well. Growing up I never knew where it came from, it was just something that we did. Now I have a new appreciation for this art form. I now know that it is part of my history, and it is something that we, as African Americans, can call our own. —HONOLULU, HAWAII

I am only nine and a half years old. I really love your book *SNAPS*. I was being insulted by a kid at school and needed a book to get back at him. So I went to a bookstore looking for a book of insults. I saw a couple of books on insults and opened them. I found all the insults boring, and I didn't even understand them. I saw the spine of your book and passed by it, not thinking it would help me. Just after, my dad saw it and said, "Could this be it?" He looked inside, and there was a bunch of perfect insults on subjects I wanted. So I bought the book, and ever since then, if anyone wants to insult me, I never worry. —COPLEY, PENNSYLVANIA

SNAPS! SNAPS! is the joke book for the nineties! I am currently trying to pursue comedy. Before this book, I had trouble thinking of an act or *routine* as some call it, but now with this new tool, I'm able to put something together. I would just like to thank you.

—FORT WAYNE, INDIANA

I just bought your fucking book last night. I read all 175 pages in just 45 minutes. I just have to say it was the most, the best book that I ever bought. I was the master cracker in my school until some prickless kids came in and took over. Thanks to this book I am back!

—NEW BRUNSWICK, NEW JERSEY

I liked your book. It was so funny. I would like to give your book an award, but I would need at least two *SNAPS* books.

—WEATOGUE, CONNECTICUT

This book was wonderful. There were actually crumbs I haven't heard before. I told my father a few while he was bench pressing. He laughed so hard he almost dropped the weights on his chest. Good going. Nothing makes him laugh. —LAS VEGAS, NEVADA

ACKNOWLEDGMENTS

THANKS TO SOME EXCELLENT SNAPPERS FROM ACROSS THE COUNTRY WHO SENT IN THEIR FAVORITE SNAPS FOR US TO INCLUDE IN THIS BOOK: Todd Alexander—Columbus, OH / Christopher Arena—New Brunswick, NJ / Derek Ansam—Honolulu, HI / Jason Atkinson—Indianapolis, IN / Boe Becker and Jon Preleski—Plainville, CT / Jaime Bertan—Mission Viejo, CA / Valencia Boson—San Diego, CA / Noah Burnett—East Palo Alto, CA / Trevor Clark—Brooklyn, NY / Adrienne Cola—Los Vegas, NV / Rick Collins—Dearborn Heights, MI / Bill Craig—Chattanooga, TN / Amanda Deaton—Trenton, OH / Chris Diaz—Sharon, PA / Jason Dixie—Fort Wayne, IN / Brandon Evans—Redondo Beach, CA / Brian L. Elam—Lecamto, FL / David France—Storrs, CT (University of Connecticut) / Damaria Green—San Jose, CA / Luis Hernandez—Bronx, NY / Carter Harris—Tolland, CT / Christian Hughes—Hopkinsville, KY / Robbie Hungerford and Travis Hawkins—Reading, CA / D. Jones—Indianapolis, IN / Lindsey Marie Jones—Bailey, NC / Chris Kofol—Bronxville, NY / Susie Keller—Cincinnati, OH / Lisa Manescu—Bethlehem, PA / Mark Mann—Ridgewood, NY / Mashadi Matabane—Capitol Heights, MD / Miguel Matos—New York, NY / Josh Maywalt—Knoxville, TN / Steve McKee—Warrington, PA / Nick Minier—Lafayette, NY / Kiyomi Mizukawa—U.S. Navy / Yandi Nunez—Hialeah, FL / Tyler Norby—Portland, OR / Cooper Pozier—Albany, GA / N. Parghi—Martinez, GA / Sean Penn—Highland, NJ / Daneton Rivera—Copley, PA / Dusty Richie—Cincinnati, OH / Matt Rader—Weatogue, CT / Chapin Strong—Granada Hills, CA / Jessica Silverthorne—Washington, DC / Monica Scott—Cincinnati, OH / Chris Tobia—New Haven, CT / Mike Tratnik—Fresno, CA / Jim Trinh—Egan, MN / Fred Wolff—Bellflower, CA.

WE THANK THE FOLLOWING (IN ALPHABETICAL ORDER) FOR THEIR CREATIVE CONTRIBUTIONS AND SUPPORT: Chris Albrecht • Atlantic Records • Tobe Becker • Bill Bellamy • David Bowden • Bill Branca • Michael Braver • Alyson Careaga • George Carlin • Dave Chapelle • Bill Chase • Barbara Cisco-White • Glynice Coleman • Nigel Cox-Hagan • Eric Davis • Dr. Dre • Jay Durgan • Traci Egan • Patrick Ewing • Fig • Kevin Fitzgerald • Gangstar • Nancy Geller • Susan Gomberg • Alan Grabelsky • Gerry Griffith • Bruce Grivetti • Guru • Peter Harring • Phil Hartman • HBO • Austin Hearst • Heavy D • Nancy Hellinghausen • Bruce Hill • Heather Humphrey • Ice-T • Jack the Rapper • Lawrence Hilton Jacobs • Michelle Jaffe • Dennis Johnson • Lisa Jones • Quincy Jones • Big Daddy Kane • Mitchell Klipper • Stuart Krasnow • Chris Kreski • David Kronemeyer • Ricki Lake • La Mama Experimental Theatre • Andrew Leary •

Michael Lewittes • Angie Li • Ed Lover • Louise Lynch • Bernie Mac • Anthony Malatino • Scott Manning • Allen Marchioni • Mary Ann McDevitt • Jim McGee • Judy McGrath • Bill Miller • Roger Mosley • Wendy Moten • MTV • Christina Norman • Andy Nulman • Noreen O'Loughlin • Bruce Paisner • David Percelay • Robin Prever • Production Partners • Sylvia Rhone • Leonard Riggio • Stephen Riggio • Michael Rudell • Rysher Entertainment • Mary Salter • Keith Samples • Scripps Howard Productions • James Signorelli • Russell Simmons • Roy Smith, Esq. • Alan Sosne • Ellen Stewart • Joel Stillerman • Caroline Strauss • Chuck Sutton • Rosemary Sykes • Dedra Tate • TOGA! • Liz Tzetzo • Suzanne Vega • Meryl Vladimer • George Wallace • Lori Weintraub • Terrie Williams Agency • Frank Wolf.

Sharon Alexander • Andre Allen • Joan Allen • Vince Anelle • Ardie • Keith Armstrong • Benny B. • Mike B • Nicola Bailey • Sean Bailey • Katisha Baldwin • Rob Bartlett • Bart Bartolomeo • Donna Baynes • Chip Bell • Lola Bell • Louis Bell • Yvonne Bell • Terrence Benbow • Big L • Big Warren • Black Filmmaker Foundation • Michael Blackson • John Blazo • Eric Boardman • Brooklyn Mike • Andre Brown • Kevin Brown • Willie Brown • Buckwild • Xavier Cadeau • J. C. Callender • Caribbean Cultural Center • Shellie Carter • Crystal Castro • Cedric the Entertainer • Donald Chapman • Ava Cherry • Bridgette Chin • Joe Claire • Lisa Clarke • Chris Cohen • Yvette Colt • Linda Coles • Joe Cooney • Diane Corder • Lisa Cortes • Sean Couch • Andre Cousins • Douglas Crew '78 • Kathie Davidson, Esq. • Pat DeRosa • Diamond D • D.K. • Albert Dotson, Esq. • Doug E. Doug • Tina Douglass • Jeanine DuBison • Barry Dufae • Adolph and Mary Dulan • Susan Duncan • Dr. Monica Dweck • Natalie Dweck • Vaughn Dweck • Patrick Ellis • Michael Epps • Nabi Faison • Shirley Faison • Diana Farmer • Fat Joe • Lord Finesse • Flex • Hope Flood • Harry Fobbs • Scott Folks • Ronda Fowler • Sundra Franklin • Diane Gaffney • David Gallen • Dianne Gibbs • Adele Givens • Dr. Steven Glickman • Valerie Graham • Carole Green, Esq. • Rona Greene • Darlene Hayes • Tanya Heidelberg • Ernie Hill • Terry Hodges • Jordan Horowitz • Lisa Humphrey • Asondra Hunter • Beverly Ivey • Waverly Ivey • David Johnson • Homer Jolly • Alonzo "Hamburger" Jones • Jamal Joseph • Sydney Joseph • Ada Keibu • William Keller • Barry Kibrick • David King • Patricia Lawrence • Rodney Lemay • Jerry Levanthal • Michael Libird • Adrienne Lotson • Persina Lucas • Mary Luthi • Uncle Jimmy Mac • Macio • Johnnie Mae • Rob Magnotti • Doris McCormick • Mercedes • Debbie Miller • Monique • Corwin Moore • Hugh Moore • Tracy Morgan • Lonai Mosley • Roger Mosley • Patrick Moxey • Mugga • Earl Nash • National Black Theatre • Kenny Nealy • John Noonan • Jim O'Brien, Esq. • Joellyn O'Loughlin • Mark Overton • Consuelo Patterson • Debbie Pender • Lewis Perlman • Al Pizzaro • Alan Potashnick • Preacher Earl & the Ministry •

Dorothy Pringle • Brett Ratner • Ratzo • Lisa Ray • Ray Ray • Mitchel Reisman • Andre Richardson • Freddie Ricks • Ray Rivera • Jack Sahl • Traci Salmon • Tunde Samuel • Cleo Sanders • Laura Sanders • Janice Schenck • Jeff Schon • Neil Schwartz • Dick Scott • Robert and Marsha Seely • Sarah Serluco • Judith Service • Beth Shelansky • Showbiz & AG • Joe Siegal • Sheri Sinclair • Rickey Smiley • Miyoshi Smith • J. B. Smooth • Jeri Snead • Somore • Special K • Rob Stapleton • Rosalyn Strain • Bob Sumner • Talent • TCF Crew • Barbara Ann Teer • Howard Thies • Ernest Thomas • Randy Tibbott • Wayman Tisdale • Ana Tolentino • Keith Truesdell • Paul Ungar, Esq. • Wilson Van Law • Michael Vann • Marta Vega • Rich Voz • Michael Walton • Theobald Walton • Monique Watkins • Janet Weiss • Marchene White • A. G. White • Doreen Whitten • Michael Williams • Hilda Willis • Ghana Wilson • Richard Winkler • Stanley Winslow • Tony Woods.

AND HUGE THANKS TO THE SUPPORT OF SOME OF AMERICA'S LEADING COMEDY CLUBS:

Uptown Comedy Club	Kevin Brown, Andre Brown	New York, NY
Boston Comedy Club	Barry Katz	New York, NY
Comedy Act Theatre	Michael Williams	Los Angeles, CA
The Townhouse	Hope Flood	Los Angeles, CA
The Funnybone	Dee Lee and Mike Bailey	Philadelphia, PA
B's Comedy Kitchen	Leslie Rodgers and Steve Maminga	Detroit, MI
Hip Hop Comedy Stop	Rushaion McDonald and David Raibon	Houston, TX
Monique's Comedy Club	Steven Imes	Baltimore, MD
The Sugar Kane Club	Charles Kane	Washington, DC
Bugsby's Spotlight-Comedy Theatre	Wendell Rush	Birmingham, AL

SPECIAL THANKS TO THE RADIO PERSONALITIES WHO HAD THE BALLS TO
INTERVIEW US:

Ed Lover and Dr. Dre	WQHT	New York, NY
Vaughn Harper	WBLS	New York, NY
Ken Webb, Jeff Foxx, and D.J. Red Alert	WRKS	New York, NY
Don Imus	WFAN	New York, NY
Howard Stern	WXRK	New York, NY
Mark Riley	WLIB	New York, NY
Mike Sargent	WBAI	New York, NY
Aaron Goldman	WNYU	New York, NY
Brian Scott	WBLK	Buffalo, NY
Rico Reed	KACE	Los Angeles, CA
Jack Patterson	KJLH	Los Angeles, CA
Donald Lacey	KPOO	San Francisco, CA
Davey D and Kevin Nash	KMEL	San Francisco, CA
Tom Joyner	WGCI	Chicago, IL
Raymond Ward	WVAZ	Chicago, IL
Kevin Gardner	WDAS	Philadelphia, PA
Carter Sanborn	WUSL	Philadelphia, PA
Rock Thompson	WAMO	Pittsburgh, PA
John Mason	WJLB	Detroit, MI
Mike Roberts and Carol Blackmon	WVEE	Atlanta, GA
Willis Johnson	KKDA	Dallas, TX
Tony Richards	KMJQ	Houston, TX
Russ Parr	KJMZ	Irving, TX
Skip Murphy	KKDA	Grand Prairie, TX
Patrick Ellis	WHVR	Washington, DC
Donnie Simpson	KPGC	Washington, DC
Hector Hanibal	WHUR	Washington, DC
Randy Dennis and Tony Perkins	WKYS	Washington, DC
James Thomas	WEDR	Miami, FL
Ed Tyll	WTKS	Orlando, FL
Chico Adams	WTMP	Tampa, FL
Jay Michaels and Randy Patterson	WHJX	Jacksonville, FL
Harold Pompey	WWIN	Baltimore, MD

Roy Simpson, Jean Ross, and Bee J	WXYV	Baltimore, MD
Tony Scott	KMJM	St. Louis, MO
Don Powers	KPRS	Kansas City, MO
Keith Richards	KJMS	Memphis, TN
CeCe McGee and Mark Evans	WHRK	Memphis, TN
T. Wright	WQQK	Nashville, TN
Lynn Tolliver	WZAK	Cleveland, OH
K. C. Jones	WVKO	Columbus, OH
Fredd E. Redd and Chris Thomas	WIZF	Cincinnati, OH
Tony Green	WQMG	Greensboro, NC
Cy Young	WQOK	Raleigh, NC
Juan Conde	WCDX	Richmond, VA
Sonny Andre and J.C.	WMYA	Norfolk, VA
Morris Baxter and Kim Nelson-Ingram	WMYK	Norfolk, VA
Chase Thomas, Stan Verret, and Cheryl Wilkerson	WOWI	Norfolk, VA
Tom Jenson and Steve Billius	KNUS	Lakewood, CO
C. J. Morgan	WQUE	New Orleans, LA
Genevieve Steward	KQXL	Baton Rouge, LA
Brian St. James	WTLC	Indianapolis, IN
Dorian Flowers	KMOJ	Minneapolis, MN
J. B. Louis	WBLX	Mobile, AL
Dave Donnell	WENN	Birmingham, AL
Mel Marshall	WVAS	Montgomery, AL
Curtis Wilson	WWDM	Columbia, SC
Dan Jackson	WKWQ	Cayce, SC
Mark Clark and Patrice Smith	WWWZ	Charleston, SC
Vince Bailey and Broadway Joe Booker	KIPR	Little Rock, AR
Paul Todd	WJMI	Jackson, MS
Pat Sheehan	WXYT	Southfield, MI
Tony Fields	WKKV	Milwaukee, WI
D. J. Berry	WLUM	Milwaukee, WI
Peter Anthony Holder	CJAD	Montreal, Canada
Angela Jenkins	KBMS	Vancouver, Canada

ABOUT THE AUTHORS

2 BROS. & A WHITE GUY, INC. is a production company formed by a producer, a comedian, and an entertainment attorney. The principals authored the best-selling book *Snaps* and introduced the word "snaps" into the lexicon. They have produced a series of *Snaps* television specials for HBO and a humorous antiviolence image campaign for MTV. The company recently coproduced a *Snaps* CD on Atlantic Records. 2 Bros. & A White Guy, Inc. consults corporations on product marketing to urban audiences.

THE PRINCIPALS . . .

JAMES PERCELAY is a writer/producer and executive producer of the HBO series *Snaps*. His background includes production on the parody commercials for *Saturday Night Live* and documentaries ranging from *The Dance Theatre of Harlem* to *The Rolling Stones*. James is former head of development at Hearst Entertainment and has produced projects for all three networks. He is a member of the WGA and currently part of a development team creating an episodic series for CBS.

STEPHAN DWECK is a prominent entertainment attorney specializing in music and television. Stephan's clients include over forty recording artists ranging from current top-forty bands on major labels to underground acts that he cultivates. Stephan represents over seventy-five currently working television and film actors. He is also counsel for organizations like The National Black Theatre and Harlem's Uptown Comedy Club. Stephan teaches a weekly entertainment law course at Baruch College and is co–executive producer of the HBO *Snaps* series.

MONTERIA IVEY is a writer/comedian, currently hosting twenty-two episodes of the PBS game show *Think Twice* produced by WGBH, Boston. Monteria is co–executive producer of the HBO *Snaps* television series and is the show's host. He is affiliated with the Black Filmmaker Foundation and hosts their live events. He performs stand-up comedy nationwide and opened HBO's '93 and '94 live *Toyota Comedy Festival*. Monteria is represented by the American Program Bureau to lecture at colleges on African American humor. For six years he was supervisor of a drop-out prevention program for Federation Employment & Guidance Service (FEGS).

We would like your comments on this book,

as well as your favorite snaps.

We will include your original snaps in our next book

and acknowledge your contributions.

2 Bros. & A White Guy, Inc.

P.O. Box 764

Planetarium Station

New York, N.Y. 10024-0539